T0300677

Before Wisdom:

The Early Poems of Paul Verlaine

Translated from French
by Keith Waldrop and K. A. Hays

 WORLD POETRY

Before Wisdom: The Early Poems of Paul Verlaine

Copyright © Keith Waldrop, 2023
The Good Song copyright © K. A. Hays, 2023

Certain of these translations have been published in *Aldus, Counter Measures, Ezra, New American Writing, Seedings, The Hudson Review,* and *The New Formalist.*

First Edition, First Printing, 2023
ISBN 978-1-954218-12-3

World Poetry Books
New York, NY
www.worldpoetrybooks.com

Distributed in the US by SPD/Small Press Distribution
www.spdbooks.org

Distributed in the UK and Europe by Turnaround Publisher Services
www.turnaround-uk.com

Library of Congress Control Number: 2023931094

Cover design by Andrew Bourne
Typesetting by Don't Look Now
Printed in Lithuania by BALTO print

World Poetry Books is committed to publishing exceptional translations of poetry from a broad range of languages and traditions, bringing the work of modern masters, emerging voices, and pioneering innovators from around the world to English-language readers in affordable trade editions. Founded in 2017, World Poetry Books is a 501(c)(3) nonprofit and charitable organization based in New York City, and affiliated with the Humanities Institute and the Translation Program at the University of Connecticut (Storrs).

UCONN
HUMANITIES INSTITUTE

Table of Contents

Translator's Introduction   vii

from *Saturnine Poems* (1866) *[KW]*

   Melancholy   17

   Etchings   25

   Sad Landscapes   32

   Woman and Cat   41

from *Wild Nights* (1869) *[KW]*

   Moonlight   45

   Pantomime   46

   The Lane   47

   The Walk   48

   Faun   49

   Still Naïve   50

   To Clymène   51

   Sentimental Colloquy   52

The Good Song (1870)   *[KAH]*   55

from *Wordless Romances* (1874) *[KW]*

   Forgotten Little Arias   85

   Belgian Landscapes   94

   Birds in the Night   102

   Watercolors   109

Translator's Introduction

THE BEGINNING OF MAY 1874, Paul Verlaine—thirty years old, in prison—learned that his wife's plea for a legal separation had been granted and that she would retain custody of their young son. Two hours later he sent for the prison chaplain and requested a catechism. Come June that same year he announced his conversion, and in August he confessed and took communion.

He had, of course, at the usual age, received religious instruction and taken communion. But already then, or shortly after, Verlaine was known to be dipping by preference into dirty books—well, probably not all that dirty, perhaps naughty, like Alexis Piron's *Ode to Priapus*—and at the age of thirteen he stumbled across a copy of Baudelaire's *The Flowers of Evil*. This is more extraordinary than it sounds; it was 1857, the year Baudelaire's book came out—and was banned. To the adolescent Verlaine those scandalous flowers seem to have revealed immediately a sort of poem he could spend his life writing. (Ten years later he attended Baudelaire's funeral.)

His fourteenth year, he mailed off to Victor Hugo the earliest of his still extant verses, "Death." The lack of an answer from the master in exile, while it may have rankled, did nothing to stop further production. He was now, and for good, Verlaine the poet, unsuccessful though he might be in everything else.

Child Wife

TO SITUATE THE VIOLENCE of Verlaine's temperament, biographers remind us of a military father, a doting mother, and a great deal of drink. The mother not only doted but was often in danger—throttled by her son from time to time or even attacked with a knife—and incredibly longsuffering. Occasionally he also pulled a knife on one friend or another who tried to curtail his drinking.

His father died when he was twenty-one. At twenty-five, he met Mathilde Mauté, sixteen, with little delay asked for her hand, celebrated her in a series of poems—*The Good Song* (*La Bonne Chanson*), his third book—and married her the following year.

It should be noted that Verlaine was generally considered—and considered himself—physically ugly, repulsive even (thus compared, by some, to Socrates). According to the memoir Mathilde wrote after his death (published twenty-one years after her own) she at first, like everybody, found him unattractive, but then, on a second encounter,

> noticed a complete change in his looks as he talked to me. His face seemed illuminated by a joy from within; his gaze, usually dark and glowing, became tender and caressing as he looked at me, his mouth in a smile. He seemed both excited and happy. At that moment, he was no longer ugly, and I thought of the lovely fairy tale of Beauty and the Beast, in which love transforms the Beast into Prince Charming.

Married, they seem to have lived happily enough for a few months. Two catastrophes helped destroy their peace. One was the Franco-Prussian war, declared 19 July 1870, three weeks and a day before the wedding. The danger to Verlaine turned out to be, not so much the Germans (he was adroit at avoiding actual combat) as the boredom of guard duty, leading him back to the alcohol and absinthe he had more or less forsworn. After the surrender of the French army, which ended the Second Empire, he supported the Paris Commune enthusiastically and, upon its collapse, found himself in jeopardy.

The other catastrophe was Rimbaud.

Drunken Boat

ARTHUR RIMBAUD WAS A year and a half younger than Mathilde. His mother had married a military man who, having fathered five children in seven years (perhaps in five visits—he never actually resided with his wife and children) stopped coming around altogether. She was deeply—narrowly—religious, and much of her emotion was invested in her offspring.

Arthur, her second son, stood out brilliantly among his provincial schoolmates who, he felt, were holding back his own development—a situation some of his teachers also recognized. Besides precocious ability in the classical languages, he was writing poems that his elders took seriously enough to point out their minor prosodic errors. At fifteen he discovered, on his own, a book by one Paul Verlaine, *Wild Nights* (*Fêtes galantes*). Obviously he had a sharp eye, like Verlaine. He sent the said Verlaine some of his poems. Verlaine was impressed—as well he might be—and not only invited the poet to come see him, but sent him the wherewithal to do so. On his arrival at the Verlaines' (who had by then moved in with Mathilde's parents) Rimbaud lacked a month of being seventeen. Mathilde, eighteen, was eight months pregnant.

And now Verlaine (not old really but, well, twenty-eight) was confronted with a brilliant adolescent versifying at full throttle—as he himself had at that age—and with unmistakable quality. Rimbaud, on arrival, handed his host his latest effort: "Le Bateau ivre." Verlaine, since his marriage, *had written no poetry*.

This helps explain (I don't mean, of course, excuse) Verlaine's slapping down his pregnant wife when she made a somewhat adverse remark about the young visitor's manners. She had for some time, in any case, been roughly treated.

Crisis

IN COMPANY WITH RIMBAUD, Verlaine began to write again. The two of them scribbled satirical squibs together and made themselves both famous and feared at fraternal poetic gatherings, including the convivial "Vilains Bonshommes" (*nasty fellows!*). Their sex life seems to have contained a measure of violence; wrist and thigh of Verlaine later revealed wounds. Wife and infant being more or less deserted, Mathilde's father settled them elsewhere.

The two poets, sometimes inseparable, sometimes appalled with, and fleeing from, each other, lived hectically in Belgium, in England... their one constant advocate Verlaine's mother. It never seems to have occurred to Verlaine that he might lose his "child wife" (his term—he had been reading Dickens), ever after declaring himself the abandoned one.

The famous crisis came on the tenth of July 1873 (less than two years from Rimbaud's coming on the scene) in Brussels. Verlaine bought a revolver, possibly with the idea of killing himself, and fired twice at Rimbaud, slightly wounding one wrist. In great despondency he and Madame Verlaine (*Maman*, note, was on hand) took Rimbaud to the hospital and later to the train station, where Verlaine made another threatening gesture—or Rimbaud thought he did and ran for a cop. Verlaine was arrested, fined, and sentenced to two years in prison.

A Career

THE FIRST BOOK BY Verlaine, *Saturnine Poems*, had come out in 1866. It has already his unique voice. With the second, *Wild Nights* (1869), we have his work up to the meeting with Mathilde. The songs to Mathilde (*La Bonne Chanson*) preceded his marriage.

The next collection of poems, centering sometimes on Rimbaud and sometimes on Mathilde and, often—as if surprised—on places he found himself, continue into the prison years. Many were published in March 1874—the author still in prison—as *Wordless Romances.*

Released from prison in January 1875, he made a speedy trip to Stuttgart to rejoin Rimbaud, but their reunion ended, at least according to the usual account, in a quarrel, apparently provoked by an attempt to convert Rimbaud, and with Verlaine lying in some weeds, kayoed. It was their last meeting, obviously not a rousing success—*except* that Verlaine carried away a manuscript of Rimbaud's (unpublished) *Illuminations.*

After Wisdom

VERLAINE'S NEXT BOOK WAS not published until December 1880. Published at the poet's expense and celebrating his conversion, it was entitled *Wisdom* (*Sagesse*). In it are a number of wonderful poems (some written before his release from prison), though it marks the beginning of a decline. His remaining years he lived a miserable, disordered life, often nomadic, frequently ill (many times hospitalized), regularly reduced to begging from friends or to beating his mother for enough to survive (and to drink)—and somehow managed to turn out a constant stream of quite distinctive poems. No longer his best, but better than those of most of his contemporaries.

Dead!

THE SUBJECT MATTER OF Verlaine's poems is often unimportant or banal. His miseries, for instance, unlike Baudelaire's or Mallarmé's, have no intellectual or cosmic resonance; they are simply gripes. And he is no thinker. The beauty of his poems is in the sound of their words and the grace of their lines: precise modulation, verbal harmony.

So it comes as no surprise that he himself declared poetry to be basically music. "Again," he says in his "Ars poetica," "music—always music!"

And (this is not the same thing) his poems have in fact been set by many composers, including Claude Debussy, Gabriel Fauré, Reynaldo Hahn. No translation can reproduce Verlaine's brilliant versification, or more than suggest its unique effects. But listening, for instance, to Hahn's "L'heure exquise"—sung, let's say, by Susan Graham—can reveal not the same, but a related glory.

His poetry was, and is, popular (in spite of the Surrealists, who, as Breton's best biographer writes, considered Verlaine to be merely Rimbaud's "insignificant other").* An attempt to enter the Academy was not taken seriously, but in 1894, on the death of the incumbent, he was elected—by a vote (of I know not what constituency) said to be overwhelming—"Prince of Poets."

Throughout his life he continued to promote the wonderful catastrophe, his lost Rimbaud, whom he celebrated as one of the "Cursed Poets" (*les poètes maudits*) in his book of the same title. Mallarmé was another—and in a later edition, Verlaine included himself.

The French government, having given Hugo a splendid send-off a bit over a decade earlier, kicked in only a pittance for Verlaine's burial in 1896.

He had entitled his last poem "Dead!"

—*KW*

---

* Mark Polizzotti, *Revolution of the Mind: The Life of André Breton* (Da Capo, 1997)

from *Saturnine Poems* (1866)

Melancholy

Resignation

Still a mere child, I dreamt the Koh-i-nor,
Extravaganza Persian and Papal,
Heliogabalus, Sardanapolus!

My desire built, underneath a gold ceiling,
Amid billowing perfumes and musical din,
Endless harems, paradises of feeling.

Cooler these days, though with ardent tendencies,
But knowing life better now, better at kneeling,
I've learned to curb my beautiful frenzies,
Albeit without completely giving in.

Well yes, the grandiose slips away: a pity,
But down with the nice, throw the dregs away.
I still despise the woman merely pretty.
As well as slant rhyme. And friends that pray.

II

Nevermore

Memory, memory: what do you want with me? Fall
Prompted a thrush through the vacant air;
Sun meanwhile, over a yellowing forest wind
Invading from the north, thrust its monotonous pall.

We were alone, side by side, we walked in a dream,
She and I, thoughts blown about, like our hair,
When, movingly, she turned to me, her voice
Golden: "Which day of your life has been the best?"

Her clear sweet voice, angelically fresh; my discreet
Smile I thought adequate reply, and certainly blest
I bowed devoutly to kiss her white hand... — Ah,

First flowers, how fragrant! as there slips
In a delightful murmur, the initial *yes*
From adored lips.

III

Three Years Later

Having passed the rickety strait gate,
I traversed the little park
Lit gently by a morning sun
That left on each flower a liquid spark.

Nothing was changed. I saw it all again:
Simple arbor with rattan chairs, rank vine...
Fountain still broadcasting a silvery plash,
Old guy trembling with sempiternal whine.

As before, the roses aquiver; as before,
Proud lilies tall and swaying in the wind.
I recognized every arriving or departing lark.

I found even, at garden end, unbent,
Veleda`, her plaster flaking — thin,
Surrounded by a stale mignonette scent.

---

*   Veleda was a prophetess during the reign of Vespasian.

IV

Wish

Ah! love-lays! those of our first successes:
Hair gold, blue eyes, flesh flowering; and then,
Breathing the scent of a body young and lithe,
Hesitant spontaneous caresses!

Are they really over, those joys,
Those artless pleasures? Alas, after regretted
Springtime come bitter winter days
Of doldrums, disgust, distresses.

So now I'm here alone, sad, and miss her,
Sad and despairing, shivering like a graybeard,
Like a poor orphan who's lost his big sister.

O for a loving woman, cuddly and mild,
Tender, dark, thoughtful, never shocked,
Who would kiss my forehead, like kissing a child.

V

Weariness

Softly. Softly. Softly,
Calm those outbursts, my charmer; remember
In the thick of love-making, often
What's best is meek sisterly surrender.

Be languid. Caress me drowsily,
Sigh for me as for an infant's sake.
Jealous clutch and obsessive embrace
Mean less than a long kiss, even fake.

But from your heart of hearts, my dear, you tell me
How wild passions sound the horn!...
Let it sound as the brute thing might.

Put your brow to my brow, your hand in mine
And swear to me now, oaths you'll break tomorrow,
And, O my little filly! we'll cry out the night!

VI

My Dream Again

Often among my dreams this strange and piercing dream
Of an unknown woman, whom I love as she loves me,
And who, each time not quite the same, still seems
Not altogether another, but understands and loves me.

Yes, understands. And my heart, clear
Alas to her alone, no longer a puzzle now
To her alone, and my fevered brow
She alone can freshen, with a tear.

Is she blonde, dark, red-head? —I don't know.
Her name? I remember it's sonorous and mild,
Like certain loved ones whom Living has exiled.

Her eyes are like a statue's eyes,
Her voice falls distant, calm, wise,
Inflected like voices loved long ago.

VII

To a Woman

To you these lines, for the consolation of your eyes
Where a dream of tenderness laughs and cries,
For your pure soul in all its goodness, to you
These lines from the depths of my distress.

For, alas! a hideous haunting nightmare
Without respite charges me in fury, folly, jealousy,
Multiplying like a pack of wolves,
Bloodying my lot in life and clinging there.

I suffer. Oh, I suffer horribly, so much
That the first howl of the first man
Chased out of Eden is by comparison pastoral

And what worries you may have, my dear, such
Are merely swallows in the afternoon sky
Of a nice albeit cooling day early in fall...

VIII

Agony

Nature, you fail utterly to move me: not one
Of your fruitful fields, not the rose-red farms
Of Sicily, nor the glory of the light at dawn
Or even the sad solemnity of a setting sun.

Art I mock, I mock also Mankind, songs,
Verses, Greek temples and the spiraling towers
Cathedrals push up towards the sky.
I cast on just and unjust a completely cold eye.

I believe in no God, I abjure and deplore
All thought, and that old irony Love
I insist on hearing about no more.

Tired of life, afraid of dying, like
A bedeviled brig, plaything of ebb and flow,
My soul heads for its inevitable wreck.

Etchings

I

Paris Sketch

The moon laid down zinc tints
    In obtuse angles.
Strings of smoke shaped like figure fives
Came dark and heavy where a rooftop slants.

Gray sky. The north wind mourned
    Like a bassoon.
Over there, some cautious, wind-chilled cat
Meowed in a weirdly strident tone.

As for me, I wandered through the night
    Dreaming of divine Plato, of
Phidias, of Salamis, of Marathon,
Under flickering eyes of blue gaslight.

II

Nightmare

I saw in my dream go by
— Like a hurricane on the strand —
Holding in one hand a knife,
An hourglass in his other hand,
    That knight

From old German ballads who
Through countryside and alleys,
From river to mountain,
Forest down to valleys,
    On a stallion

Fire-red and black as ebony,
Without bridle, bit or reins,
No whip, no heigh-ho! gallops along
Amid dull sputtering strains
    Forever! forever!

A grand hat with white panache
Shading his eyes which flare
And then flicker, as one sees
Through a fog, momentarily, the blue glare
    Of a pistol fired;

Like the wings of a sea-hawk
Startled by a stormy blast,
Now blown about by
Gusting snow, his vast
    Coat flapped in the wind,

Revealing this glorious sight:
A torso of shadow and ivory,
As in the blackness of the night
There flashed in strident cries
    Thirty-two teeth.

III

Sea Piece

The loud ocean
Mourning moves
Under the moon's eye
In constant motion,

Even as a jagged
Sinister streak
Rends the sepia sky
In a long zigzag.

And each liquid sheet
Convulsive, flying
Along the reefs
Goes, comes, shines, crying.

Up in the sky
Where hurricanes play,
Thunder grandly
Rumbles by.

IV

Nightwork

Night. Rain. Wan sky cut in strips
By tower, by spire — silhouette of a Gothic town
In open-work, softened to a background gray.
Prairie. A gallows weighted down
With hanged men, pecked apart by ravens,
Dancing uncanny jigs in the breezy night,
Their feet a picnic for wolves on the prowl.
Scattered brakes of thornbush and holly
Lift their horrid foliage left and right
Over the roughly sketched murky skein.
After which, around the ghastly naked feet
Of three convicts, comes a detachment of halberdiers
Whose weapons, shaped like harrow blades,
Gleam up against the downward spears of rain.

V

Grotesques

Their only steed Shank's mare,
Gold in their eyes all their wealth,
From ceaseless knocking about they've
Ruined their clothing and their health.

Indignant sages upbraid them,
Fools represent them as crocked;
They get raspberries from kids and
By whores they're mocked.

Well, odious they are, ridiculous,
Rather wicked they must seem,
Giving the impression at twilight
Of a continuing bad dream.

Fist clenched in freedom, strumming
The rasping strings of a guitar,
They sing through their noses songs
Nostalgic, mutinous, bizarre.

The fact is that, fastidious,
Their eyes laugh and their eyes cry
With the love of things eternal,
The long dead, gods gone goodbye.

— So go, perpetual vagabonds,
Cursed and condemned to die,
Wander waterway and chasm
Under Paradise's shut eye!

Nature joins with man
To wreak proper punishment
On a proud melancholy
That keeps the head unbent,

And avenges on you the blasphemy
Of hopes too vehement and vast,
Marking your cursed foreheads
With the storm's elemental blast.

June burns and December
Chills your flesh to the bone
As fever pierces your legs
Which sodden reeds have torn.

Everything repels you, breaks your heart,
And when death comes in its turn,
Emaciated, cold, your corpses
Even wolves will spurn.

Sad Landscapes

I

Setting Suns

Daybreak, debilitated,
Pours across the lawn
The melancholy
Of a setting sun,
Melancholy with songs
That still me until,
In the setting sun,
My heart no longer longs.
And dreams as strange
As suns, vermilion
Phantoms
Setting over shores,
File past without a pause,
File past, much like
Vast suns, setting
Over shores.

II

Mystic Twilight

Reminiscence and the dusk
Glow red and tremble as the horizon's
Ardent hope springs up
In a mysterious garden
Where profuse flowering
— Dahlia, lily, tulip, buttercup —
Proliferates along lattice-work
And thrives in sick effluvia from
Hot and heavy scents, whose poisons
— Dahlia, lily, tulip, buttercup —
Drowning my senses, my soul, my reason,
Mix in one boundless swoon
Reminiscence and the dusk.

III

Sentimental Promenade

The setting sun hurled its final ray
While wind cradled the pale water-lilies;
Among reeds the great water-lilies shone
Sadly across calm waters. Me, I made my way
Alone, taking my wound for a walk
Along the pool, among willows where
Vague mist suggested a stark
Milky-white phantom in despair,
Weeping like a river duck's prayer,
Answered by a beating of wings amid
The willows among which I made my way
Alone, walking my wound; and the winding-
Sheet of shadows drowned the final ray
Of the setting sun in these pale waves
And the water-lilies, among the reeds,
Great water-lilies on calm water.

IV

Classical Walpurgisnacht

The black sabbath of Faust (Part Two, not Part One),
A rhythmic sabbath. Rhythmic. Extremely
Rhythmic! — Imagine a Versailles garden,
    Correct, ridiculous, comely.

Roundabouts; fountains at the center; straight
Paths; marble genii; bronze marine
Deities; Venuses scattered here and there;
    Quincunxes; a bowling green;

Chestnut trees; fields of flowers outlining a down;
Here, dwarf roses someone of taste has grown;
Farther on, yew trimmed triangular. And all this
    Summer evening, the moon.

Midnight strikes, out of this courtly park is borne
A melancholy song — a dull, slow, sweet hunting
Song, like the sweet, slow, dull melancholy of
    Tannhäuser's hunting horn.

Veiled songs from distant horns, the caressed
Senses embracing the frightened soul, all
Discords drunk into harmony at
    The hunting horn's call.

Suddenly diaphanous bleached-out forms
Intertwine, which the moon makes glow
Opalescent among green-shadowed branches
    — Raffet* dreaming a Watteau! —

In languid gestures of profound despair
They intertwine among a tree's green branches,
Then, among monumental bronze and marble,
    Execute slow round dances.

— These restless specters then, are they the poet's
Drunken idea, or his regret, or his confession said?
Are these restless specters an organic rabble
    Or simply the dead?

Is it your remorse, you idle dreamer, that has led
To this horror, or your regret, or your thought, huh?
All these specters gripped by a clinging vertigo,
    Or just some mad impulse of the dead?

---

*   Denis-Auguste-Marie RAFFET (1804-1860), French painter, famous for
his lithographs of soldiers.

Never mind. They're always there, feverish phantoms
Dancing a vast mournful round, skating
Like motes in a ray of sunshine and then
    Evaporating

Moist and cadaverous, while dawn silences, one after
Another, the horns, until there's nothing to expect,
Absolutely nothing but a garden like Versailles,
    Comely, ridiculous, correct.

V

Song of Autumn

The long moan
Of autumnal
    Violins
Assails my heart
In a frail
    Monotone.

Faint and stifled
As the hours
    Toll,
I try recalling
Days gone by
    And cry,

Blown in ways
The wicked wind
    Weaves,
Here, there,
Like the dead
    Leaves.

VI

The Gloaming

At misty horizon a red moon;
The prairie in a dance of fog
Dozes in haze, while from green
Shivering reeds comes the croak of a frog;

Water lilies begin to close up;
Poplars stand tall in cluster,
Perpendicular imprecise specters;
Fireflies lend thickets luster;

Bats, waking, soundlessly
Fan the dark air in their flight;
The sky above fills with a cloudy glow
As white Venus brights up, now it's night.

VII

Nightingale

All my memories, with the squawk of
Roused birds taking wing, fall on me,
Fall with the heart's falling leaves
Around my bent trunk of an alder tree
Mirrored in the nearby melancholy flow
Of the blue river of Regret.
They fall, and then an ill
Murmur, quieted by the damp wind,
Fades by degree into the tree until
Finally nothing is heard,
Nothing but a voice celebrating Her Absence,
Nothing but the voice — languid! —
Which was my First Love, the bird
Singing still, as once, and
In the sad splendor of the rising
Moon, pale and stark,
On this dull melancholy summer night
Full of silence, full of the dark, keeps
Rocking against the sky, stroked by a breeze,
Tree that shudders and bird that weeps.

Woman and Cat

With her cat the woman played
And how marvelously one saw
The soft white hand and the white paw
Sport in the falling evening shade.

The little villainess! she hid
Under those mittens of black thread
Her murderous agate claws, unseen
But razor-like and razor-keen.

The other too put on an act
And made her steely claws retract;
Ah but the devil took no loss...

And in the darkened boudoir where
Her airy laughter rang — in there
Shone four fine points of phosphorus.

from *Wild Nights* (1869)

Moonlight

Your soul is a select territory where
Maskers and bergamaskers improvise,
Playing the lute and dancing, rather
Sadly, in whimsical disguise.

Although singing, in a minor key,
Love triumphant and life in tune,
They seem to doubt their happiness,
Their song absorbed by the light of the moon.

The moonlight, calm and sad with beauty,
Gives dreaming birds in the trees dream tones
As fountains sob in ecstasy,
Grand fountains, slender among stones.

Pantomime

Pierrot, who's by no means Clitandre,
Gulps down a jugful on the double
And finds a hunk of paté no great trouble.

Cassandra, down the Avenue,
Cannot hold back a hidden tear
For her disinherited nephew.

And this gross Harlequin gets
To kidnap Columbine
And also do four pirouettes.

Columbine dreams, given a start
To feel a heart in the wind blowing by,
Hearing voices within her own heart.

The Lane

Painted, made up as if for yesteryear, she goes
Slender in enormous ribbons and bows,
Shaded by leafy branches
Along a lane with moss-greened seats,
With her myriad affected ways
More suitable for parakeets.
Blue is her long dress with its train, the fan
Brandished in her narrow ring-burdened hand
Snickers its subjects, erotic but so vague she
Smiles, cramming details into a better dream.
— In short: Blonde. Pretty nose and what
Rosy lips, fleshed with a pride divinely
Unconscious. — Nicer, in fact, than the beauty-spot
Bringing out her eye's rather silly gleam.

The Walk

So pale a sky, the trees so skinny
Seem to smile at the bright things
We wear, which flutter with an air
Of nonchalance and flap like wings.

A breeze ripples the little lake,
And rays of sunlight diminished by
A row of lime trees that shadow the lane,
Reach us livid, all set to die.

Flawless deceivers and charming flirts,
Hearts tender but no pledges done,
We gossip deliciously while
Each lover torments his well-loved one

Whose hand uncannily knows how
Sometimes to give a whack in exchange
For a kiss on the very tip of her
Little finger, and since the range

Of such things she ranks as wild excess
She punishes, with a cold look that slips
From her eye, contradicting, as it happens,
The lackadaisy implied on her pursed lips.

Faun

An old terracotta faun laughs
In the middle of the bowling green,
No doubt portending some bad end
To what's been up to now serene:

Having led me, having led you,
Melancholy pilgrims both,
To this hour whose present retreat
Is timed to the tambourines' beat.

Still Naïve

High heels contended with long skirts
So that, depending on what wind was up,
Sometimes an ankle came in sight, usually
Well taken in! — and we loved playing dupe.

Sometimes too, under the branches, a bite
On the throat by some jealous insect troubled
Our belle and the sudden flash of white
Flesh was a feast for our foolish eyes.

Evening fell, an uncertain evening in fall:
The belles, dreamstruck, hanging in our arms,
Said softly, then, a word so wonderful
That even now I feel its awe and its alarms.

To Clymène

Mystical barcarolles,
Songs without words,
Dear, given your eyes
    The hue of skies,

Given your voice, strange
Sight to derange
And trouble the horizon
    Of my reason,

Given the unmistakable scent
Of your swanlike pallor
And your odor's
    Candor,

Ah! since your whole being,
Its subtle music, seeing
Dead angels' haloes,
    Chords, perfumes,

Beguiles my heart
To its harmony,
Its cadenced art,
    Amen, so let it be!

Sentimental Colloquy

Two figures just now crossed
The lonely old park rife with frost.

Their eyes dead, their lips clay,
Difficult to understand what they say.

In that lonely old park rife with frost,
Two specters conjuring what's lost.

— The ecstasy we felt, don't you recall?
— Now why bring such things up at all?

— Does my name still make your heartbeat go?
Is my soul permanent in your dreams? — No.

— Ah! those unspeakably happy days when
Our lips were joined! — Maybe, back then.

— How blue the sky was, our hopes as high!
— Hope has fled, bested, under a black sky.

So through old wild oats they erred
And what they said only night heard.

The Good Song (1870)

I

The morning sun now slowly warms and gilds
the rye and wheat all moist and dew-strung still,
and the sky holds close the fresh cool stance of night.
One leaves without an aim except for leaving,
walks the length of river, follows vague
gold grass, a path of lawn along the alders, aged
as air. The air is keen. Now and then a bird
with hedge's fruit or straw in beak has turned
and passed so water mirrors its long gleam,
and this is all.

    But the dreamer likes this scene
whose bright-hued softness has just now caressed
and soothed his dream of daily happiness,
and lulled his charming memories of a girl,
pale form who sings and shimmers, whirled
through the poet's thoughts, the cherished one
who holds his wishes, smiling, who's become
the Companion he has found at last, the soul
his soul has mourned and sought, today, and days of old.

II

All grace and all nuances
in sixteen years' sweet glow,
she has a child's guilelessness,
a trick, an innocent joke.

Her eyes, which are an angel's eyes,
know how (without the thought of it)
to kindle in me the strange desire
for an immaterial kiss,

and her hand, so slight
that in it a moth could hardly rest,
holds captive without hope of flight
the heart she's brought in secret.

Knowledge makes its home in her
in aid of noble love; she is
quick-witted just as she is pure:
what she asks, one must give!

And even if this foolish act amuses
her and has her laugh, pitiless,
she would be (as the muse)
gracious up to friendship,

up to love — perhaps! Who knows,
when it comes to the writer, smitten,
who would beg through her window —
audacious one! Love, a worthy award

for his song, bad or good!
But to sincerely testify,
without cloying and without false note,
to the warm wounds one suffers in love.

III

In grey and green, in dress with print of hives,
one June when I sat somber in malaise,
she came to me and smiled at my gaze
and I admired her, not fearing cruel surprise.

She came and left, came back to stay; then sat
and spoke: so low and light, ironic, bold,
that I began to feel my shadowed soul
become a glad reflection of all that;

Her voice, a chord of music, granted fine
accompaniment to that delicious prattle
of a spirit who won't guard her charming babble
as joy of heart spreads out, and is divined.

But suddenly I was, after the fray
of a revolt immediately quelled,
so rife with fervor by some fairy's spell
that still, since then, I tremble, ask, and pray.

IV

Since the dawn grows, since it's dawning here,
since, after having gone from me so long, hope consents
to turn towards me (who calls and asks her near),
since what she wants for me is this: all happiness,

it's over with, the funeral thoughts, all over
are the foul dreams, ah! Above all
the irony, the pinched lips—the words
where vacant wit would triumph over soul.

Behind as well the clenched fists, the angered brow,
the idiots, the evil, and the cruel;
behind, the vile grudge! And gone, now,
the forgetting one once sought in trashy drink!

Because I want, now that a Being of radiance
has cleared this night, the whole flood
of love from time immortal, time first;
and by the grace, the smile, and the good,

I want, guided by you, great eyes of flame,
for you to lead, oh hand where my hand trembles,
to walk steadfast on paths of moss
or on rocks and pebbles that litter the road;

yes, I want to walk in calm, upright,
with fate to guide my steps; to reach the goal
without remorse or lust, no more at odds—
this will be the happy work of our two souls.

And, lulling along the length of road,
I would sing simple airs. I tell myself
she would listen without displeasure, without doubt,
and in all truth, I want no other paradise.

V

Before you must go, pale
morning star of mine
  — One thousand quail
sing, sing in the thyme. —

Turn toward the poet
whose eyes rise, rife with love
  — One lark flits
to ride day's air above. —

Turn your gaze, be drowned
in this dawn's blue-laced zeal.
  — What joy's found
among the wide wheat fields. —

Then make these thoughts below
bring light (so far, oh! far away!)
  — Now dew's glow
shines sweetly in the hay. —

Day's dreams prick
my dear still-drowsy one...
  — Quick, love, quick,
for here's the golden sun. —

VI

The white moon
washes the boughs
as each branch
winnows the sound
of leaves, rubbed...

Oh, well-loved.

The pond reflects
in echoed mark
the silhouette
of willows, dark
where winds flower...

Dream, it's the hour.

A vast and tender
soft appeasement
now descends
from the firmament
with a single star...

Oh, exquisite hour.

VII

The landscape in the carriage window's frame
runs furiously. Entire plains
of water, wheat, tree, and vaulted sky
are now engulfed within the whirlwind's eye
which cruelly fells the telegraph poles and rends
their wires, strangely curving, as if penned.

The odor of burnt coal and boiled water
and the noise of a thousand chains uncoiled
which hold a thousand giants whipped and fowled
and a sudden prolonged cry — an owl.

— What makes me all this, when I've in my eyes
the white vision which makes my heart rise up
in joy, when the sweet voice murmurs on
and the Name so good, so noble, sonorous,
can merge, pure pivot of whirling imagery,
with the rail car's brutal rhythm — seamlessly.

VIII

A Saint within her haloed glow,
a Manor Lady in tower above,
both names that take into their tow
all words of human grace and love;

a note of gold, a sound remembered
through the woods, a horn from far away —
all wedded to the prideful tenderness
of noble ladies, yesterday;

and with all that, a charm that spawns
a fresh triumphant smile, pure
and open as the candor of a swan
or as a blushing woman-girl;

These nacreous aspects, pearl and rose,
a soft patrician whole retain:
I see, I hear such things repose
within her Carolingian name.

IX

Her right arm, with a sweet and amiable gesture,
reposes on the shoulder of her sister,
while her left arm has the rhythm of her skirt.
It's certain that congenial thoughts confer
within her eyes (so frank) and in her smiling lips
which testify to joy of spirit, intimate.
Oh! Her thought, exquisite, fine, what is it?
All lovely and all beautifully framed
for this portrait, her infallible taste chose
the best, most perfect, and most simple pose:
upright, straightforward gaze, loose hair, her dress
just long enough that she need not wear less
to hint, beneath those jealous folds, of slow
malicious charms, a foot. Those imperceptible toes.

X

Fifteen long days more and more than six weeks spent
in wait. True, of all the human anguish we have pent
within, the most doleful's that of being far, and lone.

To write, to speak of how we love; to hone
each day an evocation of the voice, the move, the eye
of the one who makes us happy; to rest, to lie
for hours all alone with thoughts of the away.
But all of what we think and what we say,
and all of what we feel of the far-off persists
in staying pale, and faithfully still sad, well-missed.

Oh! The absence! Least mild of all hurts!
To console oneself with phrases and with words,
to draw into one's mind, that vast morose
infinity, refresh her face with wearied hope
and journey back to nothing — the bitterness, the bland!
Then here, the piercing cold, a sword's thin band,
it comes, more rapidly than birds and than a shot,
and than the south-blown sea-winds with their gusts,
and on its sharpened point a poison, fine,
it comes, it's here, like arrows flung, suspicion, brine
that drips from toxic, turbid Doubt.

Can it be true? And leaning on my table, I reach out
to take and read her letter, tears in eyes,
her letter, where she's spread a sweet confession like a sigh,
could she not be distracted, caught, or drawn to other things?

Who knows? As here for me each day will bring
its slow, sad flow, a creep past withered banks of rivers.
Perhaps her lips, so innocent, now lift and purr?
Perhaps she has forgotten, her thoughts stirred?

And melancholic, I reread her words.

XI

The hard ordeal will have its end:
my heart, greet soon what hours send.

They have long passed, those days of fears
when I sat saddened, steeped in tears.

No more, dread not the day's slow climb,
my soul, again at ease with time.

The bitter words, I've read them since
and banished somber shadows' hints,

My eyes, exiled from her gaze
are thrust to dolorous duty's haze.

I'm anxious now to learn by rote
her tender voice's golden note,

All my being and all my love
acclaims the happiness to come

when my sole dream returns to stay,
my single thought, my fiancée!

XII

Go, song, with up-drawn wing
to dance before her and to tell
what faithfulness my heart flings
to her, a joyous glow, a spell.

Dissipate, holy rays,
the darknesses of love:
dull suspicions, doubt, hate —
what's here, day breaks above.

Long time, muted, stark,
do you listen? Love comes
like a lively-playing lark
to brighten skies, calm-sung.

Go, then, song sincere,
and with no regret; may
she know that she is welcome here
when she, at last, has come to stay.

XIII

Then, we spoke of this and that —
and my eyes would look to yours for what

you might hide there — and yours would flit
to mine while keeping up the chat.

Beneath the banal sense of weighted remarks
my love wandered after your thoughts, your heart;

and in distraction, when you, speaking, let
me near, I leant my ear to your secret:

for the voice (as well as the eyes of She
who makes you joyous or sad) reveals

(in spite of all efforts, morose or cheerful)
and slips to light a being's soul.

Well, yesterday I left intoxicated, in rapture:
is it a hope, vain, that my heart nurtures

as a false and sweet companion — a vain hope?
Oh! No! Is it true? Is it true — or no?

XIV

The low hearth, the dim drawn wane of lamps;
the reverie, the head leant to the hand
and eyes that lose themselves in lovers' looks.
The hour of steeped tea and close-stacked books;
the sweetened sense of evening ended, late;
the good fatigue and the attendant wait
for nuptial shadows and the deepening blues,
oh! It's this, the dream that still renews
without release, without delay it seeks,
impatient with these months, these furied weeks!

XV

I'm nearly scared, in truth, to see
(or sense) my life's become enlaced
with thoughts of you, your radiant face
which, last summer, swept my sight from me,

your image which, I will confess,
abides inside this heart (now also yours)
which is, uniquely, now absorbed
with loving you, and with your happiness.

And I'll say (excuse me if I've stalled
in telling you) with honesty (I tremble now — absurd!)
the thought that but a smile, but a word
from you has come to be my law,

and that it would require little more
than simple gestures, a whisper or a wink
to put all my being somewhere new; to sink
me into mourning for the celestial thing you are.

But rather, I see you, the scope
(whatever somber shapes we know, whatever grave
and fecund sorrows evening brings)
of all I feel: immense, sure hope

which plunges me in joy, enough
to speak to me, again, always
through drifts of sadness — there remains
this love for you. Ah, you. What love!

XVI

The blare of bars, the mud of thoroughfares,
the plane-trees flinging leaves to blackened air,
the bus, a storm of sludge and steel
that groans, ill-balanced on its grinding wheels,
and rolls its battered eyes from red to green,
the workers, bound for clubs, whose sullen stream
of pipe-smoke pushes through the glare of cops,
the roofs that drip, the walls that sweat and drop
disheveled asphalt down where sewage lies;
all this, my route — at end, a paradise.

XVII

True? In spite of the wicked and the dolts
who will not fail to envy us our joy
we will be proud sometimes, and always indulgent.

True? Cheerful and lingering, we will go
along the modest path that shows us smiling hope,
not caring whether we will be ignored or known.

Alone in love as in a dark wood, breathing
a peaceful tenderness, our two hearts
will be two nightingales who sing at evening.

As for the World, whether it will be to us
irascible or sweet — what may be its gestures? It may,
if it wants, caress us or aim its shafts at us.

United by bonds, strongest and most dear,
and moreover possessing an armor that never bends,
we will smile at everyone — we will have nothing of fear.

Without preoccupying ourselves with the goal
that waits for us, we will walk in pace,
hand in hand, with the childish soul

of those who purely love each other, true?

XVIII

We live in the infamous time
when the marriage of minds
should seal these souls as same.
Yet in such a swirling mire
twice the courage would be required
to live beneath such feeling's claim.

Confronted with what dares one on,
it will be central as days pass, days dawn,
to lift ourselves up, thrilled and blind
in the austere ecstasy of the just, a couple sure
to proclaim love with a gesture,
    to hold it proudly, as a sign!

But what need is there to tell you this?
You, all goodness. You, all smiling lips,
won't you be an advisor, too —
your sound advice, loyal and brave —
oh, child merry with thoughts grave,
to whom my heart speaks gratitude!

XIX

So yes, the day will come in summer, clear:
the great accomplice to my joy, the sun,
will — above your satin and your silk — grant one
resounding beauty to your face, again, my dear.

The sky all blue like tents pitched high and late
will tremble, sumptuous, vast, a lengthy sail
above our happy foreheads which will pale
with wanting for each other, and the wait;

and when the evening comes, the sweetened air
will play, caressing through your veils' fine lace,
and stars, so peaceful, will shift from their place
to softly smile on us, the wedded pair.

XX

I once meandered paths aside
from certainties, so sad, forlorn;
your dearest hand became my guide.

When this horizon paled, far-torn
from light and feeble hope of dawn
your gaze alone could wake the morn.

No noise, but for her step's faint song
could urge this traveler, or console,
but still your voice tells me: "Walk on!"

My heart would crouch, my somber soul
would cry, alone, bewail its voice;
but there was love, delicious, whole

to join us in its way — rejoice.

XXI

The winter has ended: the light is warm
and dances from earth to the clear bare
firmament. The saddest heart must disarm
for the immense joy, freed in air.

Even Paris sullen and sapped
seems to greet the young suns
and, as if for an immense accolade,
extends a thousand arms. For once,

for a year in my soul I have had spring,
and the green return of sweet May
brings the ideal to my ideal
as a flame surrounds a flame.

The blue sky prolongs, lifts, and crowns
the immutable azure where laughs my love.
The season is beautiful, my part is sound,
and all my hopes at last — at last have come.

Let summer come. Let come again
the autumn, and the winter. And each season
will charm me, oh, You, who tend
and give to me this fantasy — this reason.

from *Wordless Romances* (1874)

Forgotten Little Arias

I

> *A breeze over the plain*
> *Holds its breath.*
> — Favart

Ecstasy's half-heart,
Loves that tire;
Woods shudder and start
Caressed by the breeze,
Above turning leaves
A chirping choir.

Faint murmured bustle,
Twitter and buzz,
From wind-ruffled grass
The hint of a gasp...
The way, under a stream,
Mute pebbles rustle.

That soul in pain
On this sluggish plain,
It is, isn't it, our own?
Mine, yes, and yours,
Breathing meek hymns
Through tepid twilight hours.

II

I sense, amid murmurs, some
Subtle vein of voices gone
And, with glimmers of music,
Wan love and a coming dawn.

And my soul, my heart, delirious,
Become a kind of double eye,
Across a troubled day grinds out
A little air, alas, the common cry.

O my frightened Love, I'd like
To die my death alone, my way,
Balance the then and the now,
Teeter-totter away my day.

III

It rains gently on the town
— Arthur Rimbaud

Tears in my heart
Like rain on rooftops.
What pining is this
That razes my heart?

Mild ringing of rain
On pavement, on tile.
In a heavy heart
How it sings, the rain.

Tears without cause
In this disheartened heart.
What! Unbetrayed?
Mourning for no cause?

The deepest pain's
Not to know why,
Empty of love, of hate,
My heart holds such pain.

---

*   There seems no reason to doubt the authenticity of this line, though
    the poem is lost.

IV

We must, as you can see, forgive ourselves things
So as to let ourselves be happy, and whether
Or not our life has morose moments
At least, don't you agree? we can weep together.

Oh that we might, we sister souls,
Mix with our vows the childish art
Of avoiding equally women and men,
Forgetting frankly what sets us apart.

Let us be two children, let's be two girls
Stuck on nothing—by each thing stunned—even
Beneath chaste arbors paling,
Unaware how all's forgiven.

V

*Joyful irritating sound from a
harpsichord*
— Pétrus Borel

The piano, kissed by a delicate touch,
Glows vaguely in the gray and pinkish dusk,
While with a wing's light whir
An old and faint and quite charming air
Prowls, a bit frightened, in the boudoir
Scented by Her long presence there.

What is this unexpected cradle
Slowly swaddling my soul in pain?
What do you want of me, sweet playful song?
What have you come for, subtle abrupt refrain
Decaying where that window, unlatched,
Opens out across a garden patch?

VII

Sad was my soul, oh sad enough to cry.
And a woman, I tell you, a woman is why.

And my heart has found no consolation,
Not even through renunciation,

Although my heart, my soul as well,
From that woman fled like hell.

But my heart, it found no consolation,
Nothing through renunciation.

And my heart, that feels so much,
Said to my soul, Could it be such?

Could it be — was it in fact —
Really a proud exile, this sad act?

My soul answered my heart: How do we
Know but what in store for you and me

Is exile, but still this same location,
At once presence and renunciation?

VIII

In the evermore
Ennui of the plain
Uncertain snow shimmers
Like sand on a shore.

The sky is copper
That's lost its sheen.
The moon's life and death
Can perhaps be seen.

Like clouds in the sky
Float great gray oaks
Obscured by fog
In the woods near-by.

The sky is copper
That's lost its sheen.
The moon's life and death
Can probably be seen.

Rasping crows
And you lean wolves,
In this arctic wind, what
Now, do you propose?

In the evermore
Ennui of the plain
Uncertain snow shimmering
Like sand on the shore.

IX

The nightingale, perched high and seeing
his image below, thinks himself fallen
into the river. On the top limb of an oak
he fears he will drown.
— Cyrano de Bergerac

Shadows of trees on the mist-covered river
    Die like smoke blown
While in the air, in actual branches
    Mourning doves mourn.

How this pale landscape, traveler, will mirror
    Paleness of your own
And how sadly, in the high foliage, your hopes
    Weep as they drown!

Belgian Landscapes

Walcourt

Tile above brick,
What charming
Cosy shelters
Lovers pick!

Leaf and flower,
Grape and hop vines,
Serious drinkers'
Come-on signs!

Hubbub and beer
In a nice hot spot,
What any smoker
Wants to be near.

Trains at need,
Highways for the high...
For us wandering jews
Windfall speed!

July 1873

Charleroi

Up from rank fields
Kobolds rise.
How the brisk wind, it
Seems, cries...

What is that sound?
A hiss through the rye.
A thornbush lands
Some man in the eye.

Not so much houses,
More like lairs.
Smithies redden an
Horizon, like flares.

So what's going on?
Train stations blare.
Eyes strain.
So Charleroi is... where?

Sinister odor,
Just what is it?
And what is all that
Rattling like sistra?

Rough sites
Breathing our own
Human sweat,
Metallic groan!

Up from rank fields
Kobolds rise.
How the brisk wind, it
Seems, cries.

Brussels: Simple Frescoes

I

Dull green and pink
Determine incline and rise.
In half an hour lamplight
Will improvise.

From the gold over simple abysses
A gradual bloodstain seeps
Across stunted trees
Where sick birds cheep.

These autumn apparitions
With hardly a pang fail,
Monotony bleeding my dreams
Listless and pale.

II

Endless avenue
Below divinely
Pale sky.
Note that we'd be
Safe, in secret
Under this tree.

Prosperous types,
No doubt buddies
Of the Comstock sort,
Arrive at the chateau.
I'd like to be one of those
Geezers with dough.

White chateau,
Facade streaked
By a setting sun.
Fields around where...
If only our love
Could settle there!

Bar of the Jeune Renard, August 1872

Brussels: Circus Horses

By Saint Giles,
My nimble
Chestnut,
Let us be off.

— V. Hugo

Turn, turn, wooden steeds,
Turn, a hundred, a thousand turns,
Turn again, turn forever, turn
To the blare of double reeds.

The fat soldier, the maid still fatter
Bask on your backs as if at home,
Since, right here in the park today,
Their superiors are also hard at play.

Turn, turn, adorable steeds
While just outside your compass
Pickpocket eyes are peeled.
Turn to the bleat of a trumpet.

Amazing how it inebriates
To turn like this in stupid rings,
Hale in the gut, a head that hurts,
Surrounded badly by good things.

Turn, turn, cast away
Any worry about spurs
To goad your gallop round.
Turn, turn. Check dreams of hay.

So scurry, you their souls' mount:
See how night, already come,
Fails to distinguish dove from pigeon,
Far from the fair, far from Madame.

Turn. Turn! Slowly the velvet sky
Adorns itself with stars of gold.
Now loved one and lover slip away.
Turn, to a drum raucously rolled.

Fairground at Saint Giles, August 1872

Spring Tides

In the meadow, winds pick
Quarrels with weathercocks. Details
Of a deputy mayor's chateau:
Blue roof-tile and red brick
By sunlight, in endless meadow...

Like trees in a fairy tale
Wild ash and vague foliage cover
Horizons a thousandfold
Across this Sahara of the prairies:
Alfalfa, greensward, clover.

Railway coaches file by in silence
Among fields just now quiescent.
Sleep on, cows! Repose, gentle
Bulls of the colossal plain, beneath
Your skies so finely iridescent.

The train glides by without
Murmur, each coach is a salon
Where the talk is quiet and one
Can appreciate at leisure this Nature
Made as if to please Fénelon.

August 1872

Birds in the Night

1

You were never patient enough,
Understandably, alas,
Being so thoughtlessly young.
The angelic age is rough.

You've never known what's really sweet.
Well, but that's understandable,
Your being so young, frigid little sister,
Your heart has not yet learned to beat.

So here I am, full of much chaste ado,
Not exactly overjoyed, but calm,
While deploring, these ill-starred months, to be
The unhappiest man alive, because of you.

2

And how right I was you can see
When, in a bad moment, I told you
Your eyes, home of my forlorn hopes,
Hid nothing any more but treachery.

You swore then that was a lie
And your gaze in its untruth
Flared like a dying fire poked up.
Your voice formed "I love you" in reply...

We're always caught, alas, hoping we might
Manage to be happy, no matter conditions...
But that day there was a cruel pleasure
Realizing at least I had been right!

3

In any case, why should I fret or whine?
You didn't love me, the affair is over,
And preferring that nobody pity me
I'll suffer on, no coward soul is mine.

Yes, I will suffer, for love you I did! But
Suffer like a good soldier, walking lame,
Limping to eternal sleep, having loved
His fatherland that's forgotten his name.

You, once my darling, my dearest,
Although the cause of all my pain,
Are you not always my homecoming,
As youthful as France, and as insane?

4

Oh I don't want to—and, in fact, could I?—
Plunge into all this my tear-streaked gaze.
But my love, which you suppose defunct,
May be working to unseal my eye.

My love—now merely recollection, though
Marked from your blows with blood and tears,
And still, as I'm afraid will happen,
Suffering on and on till death appears—

Could be right to glimpse in you
Some not entirely cut and dried remorse
And to hear, amid sheer desperation, in your
Remembering: *oh, bad bad bad, even worse.*

5

Again I see you. I poked in at the door while
You were still in bed, seemingly exhausted.
But, you, your body light with love,
Sprang up, naked, all tears and a smile.

O what kisses, madness breast to breast!
Myself I laughed amid my tears.
Those moments, among all I've kept
Remain the saddest, and also the best.

May I never see your smile again
Or your lovely eyes as they shone there
Or, indeed, you yourself, damn you,
Appearance, nothing more, exquisite snare.

6

And again I see you! For summer dressed
In white and yellow like the flowers on curtains,
But having lost the fresh good humor
We squandered at our delirious best.

The little wife and eldest daughter
Reappeared in what you wore
And already it was our destiny that
Stared at me through the veil on your hat.

All is forgiven! And that's why
I keep, alas, rather proudly,
In memories I foist on you,
Flashes from your roving eye.

7

Sometimes I'm the unfortunate boat
Running the storm with broken mast
Seeing no gleam of hope from Our Lady,
Praying not to go down, but ready.

Sometimes it's the sinner's death I die
Who knows he's damned if he doesn't confess
And without hope of a confessor
Writhes in the Hell where he knows he will lie.

Ah but sometimes an ecstasy I share
With early Christians in the lion's jaw,
Who laugh to witness Jesus, without the quiver
Of a facial muscle or a single hair.

Watercolors

Green

Just here the fruit, the flower, leaves, branches,
Here my heart beats, only for you each beat.
Do not let your white hands break it, while your
Beautiful eyes find the simple present sweet.

I come to you damp still with dew
Flung on my brow by morning's icy air.
Allow me, tired, to collapse at your feet
Dreaming precious instants of repair.

Let me lay my head on your young breast,
Your latest kisses still echoing.
Let me breathe quiet after such fine fury
And rest a while, since you are now at rest.

Spleen

The roses were red, all of them,
And the ivy all black.

Dearest, at your least shrug
All my despair comes back.

The sky was too blue, too soft
The sea too green, the air too light.

Always I dread—such suspense!—
Your sudden atrocious flight.

I'm fed up with the glossy leaves
Of the holly, with the shiny boxtree too

And the infinite stretch of the land
And, alas! with all but you.

Streets

I

Let's dance a jig!

I loved mainly her lovely eyes,
Brighter than the starry skies.
How I loved her spiteful eyes.

Let's dance a jig!

She certainly has a way
To make her lovers pay.
But charming, I must say.

Let's dance a jig!

But I find better and better
Her kisses, longer now and wetter,
Since in my heart she's a dead letter.

Let's dance a jig!

Oh I remember, I do retain
Hours and the converse they contain.
It's the principal part of my remains.

Let's dance a jig!

Soho.

II

Down the street the gutter flows!
Making its fantastic entry
From behind a five foot wall,
Without a murmur goes
Rolling opaque and pure as well
Through calm suburbs.

The street is wide, so that
The water, sallow as a woman drowned,
Descends broad and out of luck,
Reflecting nothing but fog, even
When the light of dawn has struck
The cottages, yellowish, dark.

Paddington.

Child Wife

My simplicity you never took in at all, not
    At all, my poor girl
And, annoyed, forehead wrinkled,
    You hit the trail.

Your eyes, reflecting no unkindness,
    Unfaithful mirrors of blue,
Took on a sour angle—unfortunate sister—
    Spoiling your view.

Your little arms you wave about like
    Some hero mean but strong,
Emitting bitter cries, tubercular, alas!
    You, who were essential song.

For the rumble and hiss of storms and of the heart
    Have frightened you and—damn!
You've gone bleating to your mother
    Like a stricken lamb,

Not recognizing the clarity and honor
    Of a love brave and strong,
Joyful in bad times, grave in the good,
    Until death forever young.

An icon of fin de siècle French poetry, **Paul Verlaine** (1844–1896) was a major influence on the Symbolist and Decadent movements, and a troubled and often violent alcoholic. A book of love poems for his wife Mathilde was followed by a tempestuous relationship with Arthur Rimbaud that ended with his attempted murder of the younger poet, after which Verlaine spent two years in prison. He wrote as musically of sex and sensuality as of religious innocence and spirituality. His poems were set to music by composers such as Debussy and Fauré, and his lyricism and lifestyle inspired many generations of poets from Boris Pasternak to Patti Smith. He died in poverty in Paris at the age of 51.

Keith Waldrop is the author of more than twenty poetry collections, including *Transcendental Studies: A Trilogy*, which won the National Book Award for Poetry in 2009, and an inspired translator of French poetry from Charles Baudelaire to Edmond Jabes, Claude Royet-Journoud, and Anne-Marie Albiach, honored by the French government as a Chevalier des arts et des lettres. He has also published the acclaimed memoir *Light While There is Light* (Sun & Moon) and a collection of his collages, *Several Gravities* (Siglio). For more than fifty years, with Rosmarie Waldrop, he ran the legendary small press Burning Deck. He lives in Providence, Rhode Island, and is a professor emeritus of Brown University.

K. A. Hays is the author of four collections of poetry: *Anthropocene Lullaby* (2022), *Windthrow* (2017), *Early Creatures, Native Gods* (2012), and *Dear Apocalypse* (2009). Hays' poetry has been included in volumes of *Best American Poetry* and many magazines. In 2005, Hays earned an M.F.A. in the Literary Arts at Brown University, where she worked with Keith Waldrop. Hays teaches in the Creative Writing program at Bucknell University.

This book was typeset in Romaine 20, designed by Alice Savoie in 2020 for 205TF. It is a contemporary adaptation of a French elzevir typeface called *Romain Vingtième siècle*, which was distributed by Fonderie Allainguillaume at the beginning of the twentieth century.

The cover features a rare portrait of the young Verlaine, circa 1866. The lettering and ornamental border are inspired by the late nineteenth-century works of French architect and designer Hector Guimard, whose idiosyncratic take on Art Nouveau is most familiar from the sinuous iron canopies of the Paris Métro. Guimard abandoned this exuberant style, which he likened to flowing tree sap, for a more restrained approach after the outbreak of the First World War.

Cover design by Andrew Bourne; typesetting by Don't Look Now. Printed and bound in Lithuania by BALTO print.

 WORLD POETRY

Jean-Paul Auxeméry
Selected Poems
tr. Nathaniel Tarn

Maria Borio
Transparencies
tr. Danielle Pieratti

Jeannette L. Clariond
Goddesses of Water
tr. Samantha Schnee

Jacques Darras
John Scotus Eriugena at Laon
tr. Richard Sieburth

Olivia Elias
Chaos, Crossing
tr. Kareem James Abu-Zeid

Phoebe Giannisi
Homerica
tr. Brian Sneeden

Zuzanna Ginczanka
On Centaurs and Other Poems
tr. Alex Braslavsky

Nakedness Is My End:
Poems from the Greek Anthology
tr. Edmund Keeley

Jazra Khaleed
The Light That Burns Us
ed. Karen Van Dyck

Dimitra Kotoula
The Slow Horizon that Breathes
tr. Maria Nazos

Jerzy Ficowski
Everything I Don't Know
tr. Jennifer Grotz & Piotr Sommer
PEN AWARD FOR POETRY IN TRANSLATION

Antonio Gamoneda
Book of the Cold
tr. Katherine M. Hedeen &
Víctor Rodríguez Núñez

Mireille Gansel
Soul House
tr. Joan Seliger Sidney

Óscar García Sierra
Houston, I'm the Problem
tr. Carmen Yus Quintero

Maria Laina
Hers
tr. Karen Van Dyck

Maria Laina
Rose Fear
tr. Sarah McCann

Perrin Langda
A Few Microseconds on Earth
tr. Pauline Levy Valensi

Manuel Maples Arce
Stridentist Poems
tr. KM Cascia

Enio Moltedo
Night
tr. Marguerite Feitlowitz

Meret Oppenheim
The Loveliest Vowel Empties:
Collected Poems
tr. Kathleen Heil

Elisabeth Rynell
Night Talks
tr. Rika Lesser

Giovanni Pascoli
Last Dream
tr. Geoffrey Brock
RAIZISS/DE PALCHI TRANSLATION AWARD

Gabriel Pomerand
Saint Ghetto of the Loans
tr. Michael Kasper &
Bhamati Viswanathan

Rainer Maria Rilke
Where the Paths Do Not Go
tr. Burton Pike

Waly Salomão
Border Fare
tr. Maryam Monalisa Gharavi

George Sarantaris
Abyss and Song: Selected Poems
tr. Pria Louka

Seo Jung Hak
The Cheapest France in Town
tr. Megan Sungyoon

Ardengo Soffici
Simultaneities & Lyric Chemisms
tr. Olivia E. Sears

Ye Lijun
My Mountain Country
tr. Fiona Sze-Lorrain

Paul Verlaine
Before Wisdom: The Early Poems
tr. Keith Waldrop & K. A. Hays

Uljana Wolf
kochanie, today i bought bread
tr. Greg Nissan

Verónica Zondek
Cold Fire
tr. Katherine Silver